SUNDAY EXPRESS & DAILY EXPRESS
CARTOONS

Forty-sixth Series

ANNUAL CONCEPTS LIMITED

Published by Annual Concepts Limited, One High Street, Princes Risborough, Buckinghamshire, HP27 0AG under licence from Express Newspapers plc. Printed in Italy. © 1992 Express Newspapers plc. ISBN 1-874507-05-8

£3.50

FOREWORD

BY

ERIC

SYKES

Being asked to write this foreword is like Johann Sebastian Bach asking me to turn the pages while he plays. Sadly Johann is no longer with us but thank God Giles still manages to turn out his masterpieces.

We all have or have had, or known, someone with relations similar to his family. Incidentally dietitians will be amazed to learn that Grandma although she eats plenty of what she likes hasn't put on a pound in weight for nearly fifty years. But then I don't want any of them to change because to me they are a microcosm of all the best of Britain in the last century: the church, pompous old vicar, the pub landlord and the regulars, the streets and homes, it isn't just nostalgia, it is now. Laughter is a good feeling and Giles engenders more of this therapy in one cartoon than most television comedy shows evoke in half an hour and this is no accident: there is a depth and a wealth of understanding in each brilliant creation. And here we are with another December upon us. No longer it seems do we have robins and thick white snow for the festive season, nowadays we are more likely to be lolling in the back garden in seventy degrees of sunshine, but as long as we can have Giles Christmas Annual beside us, a pint of good ale and a white hanky knotted over the bald patch we shan't do too badly.

Eric Sykes

Because of a long spell in hospital Giles apologises for having to draw from the past to compile an annual this year.

Starting with a section on the family.

"Awake, O Lord of the Manor, 'tis Father's Day and thou shalt do no work all day. Just like the other 51 Sundays in the year."

Sunday Express, June 19th, 1966

"Hold it, Dad—Auntie Ivy hasn't quite gone yet."

Daily Express, December 28th, 1967.

"'You, of course, had to be different. You had to go and pick the Judge up by his ears."

Sunday Express, February 11th, 1968

"They're signing a two-day truce with Grandma. They won't play any Christmas jokes on her if she promises she won't sing."

Daily Express, December 24th, 1968

"Grandma, you must let Vera vote for whom she chooses."

Daily Express, June 18th, 1970

Sunday Express, December 27th, 1970

"It is most certainly not time for Service yet madam—I suggest a junior member of your family has put your clock a few hours forward instead of one hour back."

Sunday Express, October 31st, 1971

"I'll tell you why we're suspicious—because this is the fifth fiver you've changed this morning for a penny Oxo cube."

Sunday Express, November 28th, 1971

"You might have let him hit <u>one</u> as it's Fathers Day."

Sunday Express, June 18th, 1972

"She'll give you 'Sportsman of the Year' if you miss."

Daily Express, November 14th, 1972

"As a matter of fact I did read that a doctors' journal said that swearing is good for you—but not that good."

Sunday Express, April 14th, 1974

"As a matter of fact we do not think this is better than taking one of those chancy holidays in the Med."

Sunday Express, July 28th, 1974

"Mum! Grandma's gone down behind the piano."

Daily Express, December 28th, 1974

"Of course Mummy loves you—and there's no question of us being in a mad hurry to get you back to school."

Daily Express, September 9th, 1975

"Mother, did you remember to tell the boys to save their bath water for the garden?"

Sunday Express, May 9th, 1976

"You'll have to find somewhere safer than the top of the cupboard to hide the presents—they've found Dad's."

Sunday Express, December 12th, 1976

"When I said build them a tree-house to keep them quiet, I didn't mean to include room-service."

Sunday Express, July 24th, 1977

"Here it comes again—they didn't call off racing just for a bit of frost when she was a girl."

Daily Express, February 20th, 1978

"We chained Grandma up to celebrate the Suffragettes' anniversary and Butch has swallowed the key."

Sunday Express, July 2nd, 1978

"Right—on the show of hands Sebastian gets a reprieve—one of you go to the shop and get six large tins of corned beef."

Sunday Express, December 17th, 1978

"Dad, Mum says would you like a mince pie while we're waiting for the fire brigade?"

Daily Express, December 24th, 1979

"Dad, you know the Consumers Association said a goose is a better guard dog than a dog?"

Daily Express, November 24th, 1981

"You're not sending him back to Harridges to change them all on his own."

Daily Express, December 30th, 1982

"Grandma's been a great help. She's packed all the presents but forgot to label them which one's which."

Sunday Express, December 18th, 1983

"Like last year, Butch, forget walkies for a few days after his marathon."

Daily Express, May 15th, 1984

"There you are! You didn't think we would let you spend Father's Day on your own."

Sunday Express, June 16th, 1985

"He does that every time British Rail put their fares up."

Sunday Express, November 24th, 1985

"Her horse fell at the first fence, our cricketers are a pain in her neck, so she's off to pastures new."

Sunday Express, April 6th, 1986

"Grandma, we don't mind you helping the neighbours clear up their rubbish for a fiver, but we do mind you sweeping it into our garden."

Daily Express, October 20th, 1987

"You don't encourage your dad very much telling him that's more than he's scored in his whole life."

Sunday Express, May 8th, 1988

"Stand by for tidings of good cheer from the neighbours—Dad's just blown every fuse in the road."

Sunday Express, December 11th, 1988

"I can't wait to see my old man's face when I tell him he's got a couple of Chelsea buns for dinner instead of roast beef."

Sunday Express, June 3rd, 1990

"Now the war is over I assume you have decided to risk the perils of travel and give us a look."

Sunday Express, March 3rd, 1991

A section on
HOSPITALS

"I came in 'ere to have my duodenal out, not to muck about playing Father Christmas to this pack of malingerers."

Daily Express, December 21st, 1965

"I think she heard Harry saying doctors don't need more money nor don't nurses."

Sunday Express, May 8th, 1966

"Oi! Before you go. . ."

Daily Express, August 23rd, 1966

"Matron hasn't chained herself to the railings to support our cause. I put her there for changing my day off."

Sunday Express, April 27th, 1969

"Don't come whining for our custom back when your damn strike's over."

Daily Express, August 26th, 1969

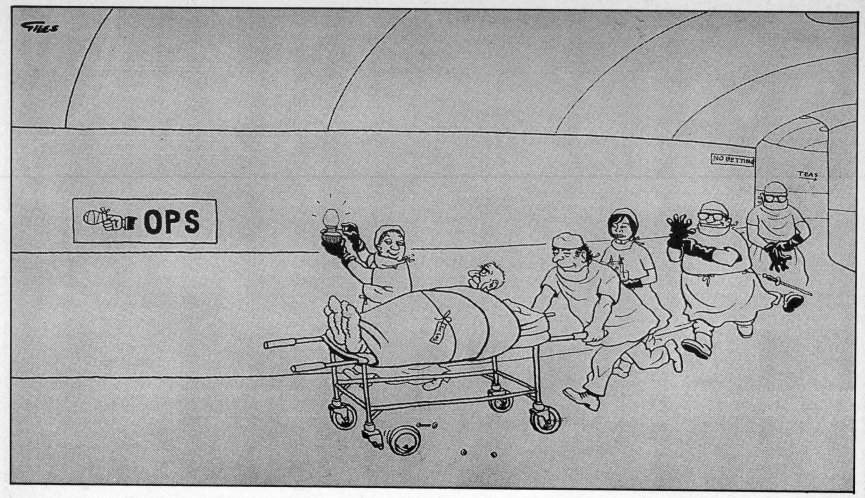

"Just in case of power-cuts, Mr. Wimple—we can't have Doctor whipping out all the wrong bits and pieces, can we?"

Daily Express, December 10th, 1970

"Which goes to prove that even if you don't think they're all little Florence Nightingales don't let them hear you say so."

Sunday Express, July 11th, 1971

"As you've been hanging around here for the last twenty years with your grumbling appendix I doubt if Doctor will classify you as an emergency."

Daily Express, October 9th, 1975

"Everybody up! Decorations down! And I warn you we're not very happy with our wage settlement."

Sunday Express, January 6th, 1980

"Something wrong with this strike—I'm working twice as hard as I do normally."

Daily Express, August 12th, 1982

"Well, that's taken care of your ambulance—telling them you knew they'd have to give way in the end."

Sunday Express, November 7th, 1982

"Great! Here cometh the plumber who charged me £75 to come and look at my burst pipe."

Daily Express, January 20th, 1987

"I'd quit this underpaid job if I wasn't dedicated to scrubbing your sweet little neck every morning."

Daily Express, April 9th, 1987

"Just turn your back for a few hours strike and they're off."

Sunday Express, January 10th, 1988

"Went head over heels giving One an extra special curtsy."

Sunday Express, September 2nd, 1990

A section on
FARMING

"It may have been a rotten harvest, but I've improved my breast stroke."

Sunday Express, October 3rd, 1965

"He's got a point—there isn't one that says 'No Fatstock'."

Daily Express, December 7th, 1965

"I know one farm worker who's been a special case around here for years."

Daily Express, February 24th, 1972

"My Maisie isn't going to like me taking home one of his flaming calves every week in lieu of my pay increase."

Sunday Express, November 10th, 1974

"Farmer says that's your lot and he'd like 'em back after the service."

Sunday Express, September 28th, 1975

"At the risk of running into touble with the Sex Discrimination Act, your presence is required in yonder meadow."

Daily Express, December 30th, 1975

"You'll have to do something about your weight, Thomas, potatoes are very fattening."

Daily Express, January 22nd, 1976

"Would you mind telling your wife to air her grievances on price increases to Mr.Peart and the Common Market and not to me."

Daily Express, March 8th, 1976

"Your little joke about 'Water, water, everywhere but not a drop to drink' didn't make him laugh, Harry."

Daily Express, August 24th, 1976

"There's another reason why you're not allowed to sell that champion bull before the end of the show—it isn't yours."

Daily Express, December 7th, 1976

"I see they gave you a good spread in the papers yesterday."

Daily Express, September 16th, 1977

"Blooming cheek! We all bought you a drink only last week to celebrate *your* pay increase!"

Daily Express, October 31st, 1977

"Don't take it personal, Sir—he do that to anyone who pats his head wearing a rosette."

Sunday Express, April 29th, 1979

"I just heard your boss say he's going to trade you in for a computerised, air-conditioned, articulated tractor."

Daily Express, December 4th, 1979

"Verily I say unto you, if you drop that bleeding spanner on my nut once more . . ."

(Archbishop of York deplores TV violence. . .)   *Daily Express, February 26th, 1980*

"Watch it, boy! They expel
us for that sort of lark."

(Students banned for sharing beds)

Daily Express, March 6th, 1980

"Here comes your missus—I think she wants a chat about you thinking of turning the farm into a golf course."

Daily Express, May 20th, 1982

"Petrol up another 5p — don't go down to the pub in the Rolls, dear, or they'll all be hollering for a rise."

Sunday Express, September 12th, 1982

"On the other hand, if you don't let me through with my sheep you aren't going to get very far either."

Daily Express, February 12th, 1985

"Who's going to tell him his country cottage is about to be replaced by a bingo hall and a block of high-rise flats?"

Daily Express, February 12th, 1987

A section on
BOATS

"We was sailing close hauled on port tack, wind variable to Force 10, suddenly I says 'Gybe ho!' Then bang! 'That's handy' my mate says."

Daily Express, January 4th, 1966

"He spent all his holiday painting the name on his boat—I hadn't the heart to tell him."

Daily Express, April 12th, 1966

"Captain doesn't know it, but one more able seaman's joining the strike at midnight. Bang on the dot."

Sunday Express, May 15th, 1966

"Sorry, Sir—but I fear this is one of the rare times when sail must give way to power."

Daily Express, August 25th, 1967

"I told you a small open boat was false economy. We should have had the one with the cabin."

Daily Express, January 11th, 1968

"A plague on the Ford women strikers. Until now the women have always done the rowing in this family."

Sunday Express, June 16th, 1968

"Veronica, please don't emphasise your dislike of sailing by calling members of the Squadron 'Slimy things that crawl with legs upon a slimy sea'."

Sunday Express, August 3rd, 1969

"Bring that thing in right alongside or it will be more than your rum ration you'll be losing."

Sunday Express, August 2nd, 1970

"This anonymous note saying you have a bomb on board—we have reason to
believe it was sent by your wife who isn't very keen on sailing."

Sunday Express, May 30th, 1971

"Ah, well, if they won't let us have a motor bike till we're seventeen, there's always the sea."

Daily Express, July 8th, 1971

"Mind if I check your gear for bombs—some of them in this Club'll do anything to win a race."

Sunday Express, May 21st, 1972

"Obviously a sailing type himself—the way he told us to push off."

Daily Express, January 4th, 1973

"You say you're running a Get-you-to-work service from South London to Westminster? Who's your navigator?"

Daily Express, March 9th, 1973

"Your wife nailing you and your boat up for Easter is hardly a case for calling the RNLI."

Daily Express, April 24th, 1973

"Whoops! There go your chances of being selected for the Admiral's Cup."

Daily Express, July 3rd, 1973

"Eggs! Super! The galley slave will soon rustle up something for everybody."

Daily Express, August 6th, 1974

"I am NOT streaking in front of the Royal Yacht!"

Daily Express, August 8th, 1974

"Funny, it looked much bigger at the Boat Show."

"I appreciate that if we're nationalised you will expect to be addressed as Marine Repair Consultant. But in the meantime, pass me that bloody hammer."

Daily Express, November 19th, 1976

"With crews like mine, no wonder they sail round the world single-handed."

Daily Express, September 5th, 1977

"When I asked you where you would be putting your cross I was asking a perfectly civil question."

Sunday Express, April 15th, 1979

"As long as you share his great British passion for sailing, its beauty and its horizons—
you should have a reasonably happy marriage."

Sunday Express, January 4th, 1981

"There's only one more Bank Holiday this month for a long weekend on the boat."

Daily Express, May 5th, 1981

"It would not only cost half the price to build in Japan—it would be half the bloody mess!"

Daily Express, July 29th, 1982

"I wasn't complaining about us being late getting in the water—
I simply said the nights start drawing in again this month."

Sunday Express, June 2nd, 1985

A section on
POLICE

"We're parked on a double yellow line."

Daily Express, December 29th, 1970

"Over 21!"

Daily Express, May 27th, 1971

"Watcha, Bertie—considering there is only one policeman for every 500 people in Britain you're a very lucky man. I am about to give you my undivided attention."

Daily Express, June 17th, 1971

"Five past two! This is a raid."

Daily Express, June 29th, 1971

"May I mention, with the greatest respect, Madam, that you have just knocked my Sergeant base over tip."

Sunday Express, February 25th, 1973

"It's very nice of you to agree with Her Majesty's tribute to our being overworked, undervalued, never overpaid—but I'm still going to book you."

Sunday Express, June 2nd, 1974

"Morning Sir. How about starting the week with being in charge of an offensive weapon, parked in a No Waiting area?"

Daily Express, June 17th, 1975

"Ernest, you did post that letter to my MP demanding the Police get a substantial wage increase immediately?"

Sunday Express, October 16th, 1977

"Three shop-lifting, two drunk and disorderly."

Daily Express, December 12th, 1977

"I've told the hospital we've got an ambulance driver fallen head over tip—want to hear what they said?"

Sunday Express, January 21st, 1979

"That one will go far—booked the Chief Constable for lingering with intent outside police HQ."

Daily Express, April 3rd, 1979

"This gentleman complains that you flew low over his nudist camp and stuck a parking ticket on him."

Sunday Express, September 2nd, 1979

"It's not often I see eye to eye with chief constables."

Daily Express, October 30th, 1979

"How come it's all right for Brighton, but in Eastbourne you end up in the nick?"

Daily Express, April 3rd, 1980

"Hi, Dad—want to see some erotic Polaroids of you dancing at the Carnival before Mum sees them?"

Daily Express, August 26th, 1980

"You, you and you—in here. You, you and you—hold on! They didn't tell us
they were sending any from Holloway."

Sunday Express, October 19th, 1980

"We can't make a cup of tea like they do in the Scrubs'."

Daily Express, October 23rd, 1980

"Yes, there are a lot of little comforts I shall miss when we go back to the Scrubs."

Daily Express, January 15th, 1981

"Don't go away son—me and my mate are just going to have a consultation
whether to thump your head or kick your backside."

Daily Express, November 26th, 1981

"The accused then said: 'How about a couple to take home for the wife?'
Thereby committing an act of bribery and corruption."

Sunday Express, July 25th, 1982

"You say the lady kissed your head under the mistletoe thereby causing you sexual harassment?"

Daily Express, December 21st, 1982

"Here comes one of 'em without a seatbelt—cover me, I'm going in."

Sunday Express, January 30th, 1983

"I think they're fascinated with your new image since they read you're all drunken racist bullies."

Sunday Express, November 20th, 1983

"I only said, 'You wouldn't happen to be one of those Kissogram cops?' "

Daily Express, November 25th, 1985

"Grandma ordered the escort—wants to make sure her pools get posted."

Daily Express, January 23rd, 1986

"Remember me? I got three years for helping you with your enquiries."

Daily Express, February 2nd, 1989

(Headline: Police replace prison officers.)